SOUTH SUDAN OUR DREAM COUNTRY

A Strategy for Peace Building

BY

Drasi Bua Caesar

This book, *"South Sudan Our Dream Country"* is a step in the right direction.

It is said that if you do not know where you are going, any direction will take you to any destination.

There is nothing as important as having a common vision that unites and rallies people in pursuit of it—a vision that people are patriotic about and ready to defend at any cost.

Rev. Dr. Drasi has highlighted a number of valuable issues to attain the South Sudan that is Our Dream Country. For example, issues of forgiveness, embracing humility, thinking right, stopping revenge, and embracing love among others. If these issues as elaborated in the book are embraced strongly from the heart by South Sudanese at all levels and from all walks of life, it will without doubt result to the South Sudan which is Our Dream Country. We all dreamt for a prosperous, democratic, and peaceful South Sudan.

It goes without saying that a vision of a better tomorrow for South Sudan should dictate how we behave and conduct our affairs. Without drastic changes in our mindset and behavior as clearly articulated by the weighty issues discussed in this book, we cannot attain the South Sudan which is Our Dream Country. As always said by many, insanity is doing the same thing but expecting a different result from it. But if we practice the basic issues pointed out in the book, with sincerity we can confidently expect a different result— the South Sudan which is Our Dream Country. I promise you, it would be a prosperous, democratic, and peaceful country.

Many South Sudanese after the short euphoria experienced during the July 2011 independence have become so disillusioned and dissatisfied with the current affairs of things in their young nation. Hard and difficult questions are being asked by many of the citizens with no clear and satisfying answerers in place. As an anonymous writer pointed about: "Dissatisfaction and discouragement are not caused by the absence of things but the absence of vision." This saying resonates what King Solomon stated in the Bible that without vision, people perish (Proverbs 29:18). In the year 2012 during the celebrations of the first anniversary of South Sudanese Independence, Ambassador Princeton Lyman—the US Special Envoy for Sudan and South Sudan asked the question: "Is there a need for a new vision for South Sudan? "An answer to that question is long overdue. Though for sure, South Sudan needs a new vision. Rev. Dr. Drasi on his part made a valuable attempt to answer the question in this timely book – South Sudan Our Dream Country.

Rev. Dema James Marchello

Senior Pastor

International Christian Assembly (ICA) – Juba, South Sudan.

Friends; we are called human beings – beings that are moral, rational, intuitive and responsible. We are created with virtues of: love, empathy, benevolent, sympathy, peace, forbearing and joy. Our problem is how we can use these virtues for the good of ourselves and others.

And here is the guide for right action. Train your thoughts, words and actions on positivity which is seasoned with love, peace, truthfulness, sincerity, empathy, benevolence and selflessness. Learn to enjoy the favor of other people starting from your family, neighborhood and beyond. Spend time to learn new graces, while dropping off the old traditions. Choose to utilize virtues that make love, peace and unity.

Friends, in unison learn to say: enough is enough to quarrels, profanity, arguments, untruthfulness, hate speeches, bitterness and revenge. Know that in life you can't change another person but only yourself. So stop hurting others and they too will stop hurting you. Accept and invite your opponents for a cup of tea, coffee and a bottle of soda. Always choose to love and forgive.

For the last 50 or so years you have been in hostility but with no gain. Instead you and your so called enemies registered loses upon loses. Why do you keep on such a course, rather than a change of direction, set a new pace for love, justice and peace!

Put away all the reasons for your fighting. Try to do it now and immediately peace will come to our land! Love wins, self-sacrifice buys. Hate destroys. Selfishness robs. Power controls on your side but on your opponents' side it builds resistance. You can control and oppress for a season, but resistance can go for generations that is why love is the best seller and buyer, nothing bypasses it or even go above or below it. Learn to respect other people and their properties, in-turn; they will respect you and your property.

Rev. Dr. Drasi Bua Caesar

Email: buadrasi@outlook.com
       buamugu@gmail.com

CONTENTS

INTRODUCTION: THE LEADING QUESTION

This book is written as a guide to the process of peace building in South Sudan. Nonetheless, its principles go beyond South Sudan to help other nations of similar problems. So the leading question for South Sudanese is:

WHAT KIND OF COUNTRY DID SOUTH SUDANESE DREAM OF?

ANSWER: THE SOUTH SUDANESE DREAMT OF...

A family is a basic social unit consisting of parents and children, considered as a group that dwells together, forming a household under one head.

A home is a permanent place where a person or persons live in one place, have rest and daily activity. A country is a large home with different people that contribute to its development and serenity.

A 'family' and a 'home' are two different words. When used together they imprint sense of a 'nation.' South Sudan is our family – a big family and a home for all who live in it.

> A home is a permanent place where a person or persons live in one place, have rest and daily activity.

This concept may be difficult to perceive even though it is the truth. We don't need to think of a family as we always do. That it is a smallest unit of society or a small group of people in one house, which sets the basis for our community and nation. Though true to think like that but that is only where it begins. When it grows from there it becomes a large group of people we can call a country.

Why is a family home important?

1. It provides natural identity

Natural identity is a person's distinctiveness acquired at birth. It accords a person with a sense of belonging. In this sense, natural identity or individuality is not legally ascribed or prescribed by writing a will. Instead it is determined by God. Therefore it is important to know that God who determines people's belonging and individualities also has a reason why a person must be born in a particular family and to particular parents. South Sudan is therefore our family home because it provides us with natural identity.

2. It provides security

This simply means that a person growing or staying in his own country has a full sense of safety from external threats. Why? Because in a family home a person is respected, valued, loved with full rights of everything in the family. It is a similar thing in a persons' own country; no one is supposed to mistreat or call him an illegitimate or a foreigner.

On the contrary, a person who stays away from his father and mother's original family is ever insecure and unhappy. He is hypersensitive. His level of fear is high and will have low morale with constrained creativity. As an adult, we all know that a child raised with conditional love outside his parents' family cannot do much due to fear that someone else may not approve his work. The fears of failure and rejection, caused by destructive criticism in his/her early childhood will be the root causes of his/her loss. For most people, their fears govern their lives. Everything they do is organized around avoiding failures or criticisms. They think continually about playing it safe, rather than striving for their goals because they seek security rather than opportunity. That's how importance it is to have a country as a family home.

3. It guides its members to discover their purpose for life

"Train a child in the way he should go, and when he is old he will not turn from it" (NIV, Proverbs 22:6). The word of God introduces parents to their first task towards, which is to train children concerning life. That is to teach children what they must know and prepare to do

when they become adults. An ideal family provides training for a child about the child's purposes in life and how he can conduct himself in achieving his purpose.

Many children born outside wedlock and not in families do not know the reasons why they exist, because there are no people to train and guide them in discovering their purpose. Such children grow up without knowing their purpose in life. Sadly, that is why many children who grow up outside good family influence become criminals.

4. A Family home provides core values

Values are moral principles that guide decisions and they are part of a family's culture. All cultures whether in a family, tribe or country fall under one of this three: Theonomous, heteronymous and autonomous. As a way of life, culture that has good moral values train children in that family to grow-up with high morality. Both in a family and society, people exhibit the values they learn there. Those who consider their values as worthy get committed to it even to the point of suffering.

It is the responsibility of various family members to introduce their young members to the family's core values. The earlier the children learn these values, the better.

> As a way of life, culture that has good moral values train children in that family to grow-up with high morality.

Learning values early enough means, by the time a child become an adult, he should have already known right thoughts, attitudes and actions to take towards others. By doing this, a child is safe from misleading patterns of living. Therefore, in a similar way, a nation that sets laws and practices them will have law-abiding citizens. These law and orders make every citizen to be responsible and accountable.

Tribal connectivity is a concept borrowed from spider web. It emphasizes the fact concerning different people living together in one accord as does a spider web. A spider web is linked together with one thread; that one thread provides strength and identity to the entire web. In a similar way a country like South Sudan is one but with many tribes. What then unites the different tribes is the soil, the geographical portion allocated to the people of this part of African region called South Sudanese.

In actual sense, all South Sudanese bear one identity – South Sudanese. This is the tribal connectivity. These people who speak different dialects live together with tolerance, love and harmony, because they respect the soil that linked them; the soil that gives them   strength and uniqueness.

Every tribe therefore, settled on this soil as a home, while appreciating God for His great gift.

> A spider web is linked together with one thread; that one thread provides strength and identity to the entire web.

One attractive fact about this connectivity is that, it does not undermine people's diversities in their cultures.

Instead, it enhances and promotes them by allowing every tribe to practice their socio-economic activities as well as preserve their physical features.

It is vital reality to understand that a land is a gift from God to one people group or another. Such act of God demonstrates His love and favor for a particular people group, which calls for respect; nobody needs to temper with it.

In the book of Acts we read that *"...God made the world and everything in it ... from one man he made every nation of men, that they should inhabit the whole earth and he determines the times set for them and their exact places where they should live ..."* (NIV, Acts 17:24-26).

The oneness of the different ethnic groups in South Sudan is a plan of God. It's not a mistake from the colonizers of the then Sudan. God's plan is that every one of the ethnic groups should live together in peace, harmony, love and unity.

Ways of living in harmony

1. Inter-Marriage

Inter-marriage is one of the means that makes different tribes in South Sudan connect to one another. Over the years, many South Sudanese tribes have inter-married. These inter-marriages tied individuals, families, clans and tribes to each other. For example, many Bari young men and women got married to the Madi and vice-versa. Likewise, many Nuer young men and women got married to the Dinka tribesmen and women.

To say a little more about these two ethnic groups for the sake of emphasis, the Dinka and the Nuer share common borders and therefore have some cultural similarities. They are of Nilotic origin, characterized by their physical features of being dark and tall. Their livelihood largely depends on cattle and subsistence farming.

While the Dinkas and Nuers could both be categorized as pastoralists, they are unlike other pastoralists who constantly move for the search of water and pastures; these two communities only move twice a year. Between December and January, the water sources around their permanent establishments dry up and they are forced to move to the swampy areas along the River Nile. Their second movement is between May and June when they return to their permanent estates as the rains start to fall.

Therefore, in many aspects, the Dinka and the Nuer are *brothers* who can only be distinguished by language and traditional markings. In fact, Dinkas who directly share the border with Nuers such as the Hol in Duk Padiet, Nyarweng in Duk Pawel, the Dinka Ngok and some Dinka of Bahr El Ghazal, share the same traditional marks and speak each other's languages. It is very important to note that this *Dinka and Nuer brotherly relationship is reinforced by intermarriages.*

Through these inter-marriages, different tribes have their own blood daughters in the land of the other tribes.

These daughters, some of them, are blessed by God to bear children, whom the tribes call their nephews and they call the relatives of their mother, uncles, aunties and cousins.

By the time western colonial powers came to the soil of South Sudan to introduce civilization and border demarcations, South Sudanese people were already linked together by their shared borders.

Therefore, these individuals, families, clans and tribes are all related to one another, because inter-marriage initiates them into new blood bonds of relationship. This needs to be treasured, respected and valued in such a way that the two tribes support each other in every way possible.

2. Neighborhood

The sixty-four tribes of South Sudan share borders with one another, and this can be dated back to ancient times. By the time western colonial powers came to the soil of South Sudan to introduce civilization and border demarcations, South Sudanese people were already linked together by their shared borders.

As neighbors to one another, ethnic groups had respect for one another in various spheres of life. Such ties conveyed – and still do – the sense of unity, harmony, tolerance and deep respect for each other. Whenever disputes arose between two tribes, they were quickly resolved mutually without magnifying or politicizing the issue. That is why the Bible says, *"Do not move an ancient boundary stone or encroach on the fields of the fatherless, for their defense is strong: he will take up their case against you"* (NIV, Proverbs 23:10-11).

God one time spoke to prophet Hosea, that He would bring calamity on leaders who moved ancient border stones. He says, *"Judah's leaders are those who move boundary stones. I will pour out my wrath on them like a flood of water."* (NIV, Hosea 5:10-11). The question is: how many boundary stones have been removed by land-grabbers? The Lord God is solemnly warning those who for one reason or another encroached into the land of other people.

3. Sharing cultures

Tribes which border each other also share some of their cultures with one another. The common shared part of culture is language. We know that language is a sign of identity. When different tribes learn one another's dialect in their neighborhood, that act of speaking somebody else's language brings the sense of belonging to one another, love and unity. Additionally to that, it is also a sense of recognition.

For us to get a lasting peace we must…

1. Accept our differences in the country

"… As God's chosen people…clothe yourselves with compassion, kindness, humility, gentleness and patience … Bear with each other and forgive whatever grievances you may have against one another. Forgive as the Lord has forgiven you…" (NIV, Colossians 3:12-14).

Human differences display the wisdom and unlimited skillfulness of God, who deliberately chose to design uniqueness into every individual person. Both nuclear and extended families have different members who differ in personality, in physiology, in behavior, in talents, in hobbies, in making choices for life partners and other affiliations. This is to say, there are so many areas in which people that are in one family or community or nation, are nonetheless different.

Some differences are human made, while others are innate; things a person is born with.

But the great truth concerning these differences is that, they are not meant to divide people or discriminate one from another.

But the great truth concerning these differences is that, they are not meant to divide people or discriminate one from another.

There is a perception that differences exist for the negative i.e. discrimination, oppression and undermining other people. But this is false. It must be discarded!

For example, in South Sudan, there are two main differences which have been misunderstood and therefore misused or abused. We must clearly understand the purpose of being in different tribes and overcome the differences that come along with them.

2. Change the attitude of Tribalism

A tribe is any aggregate of people united by its ties of descent from a common ancestry, which forms a community and shares one culture. Biologically, a tribe is a taxonomic category that ranks above genes and below family. Tribes are normally distinct from one another, either by the appearance of the people or in the dialect the people speak. Tribes constitute of social divisions in a traditional society. People of one tribe also share common socio-economic activities as the culture demands.

From the above descriptions, we can deduce that all the tribes and every person in them are of the same value regardless of
their sizes.

The uniqueness of one tribe to another is not its size but its cultural beliefs and activities.

This means that, God alone determined to which family, clan and tribe we were born and belong.

Yet, even this should not bring comparison of their value and quality, rating one good and the other bad.

One more fact about 'tribe' is that, a person does not apply to be born in the tribe of his or her choice. We all found ourselves born in the tribes to which we belong. This means that, God alone determined to which family, clan and tribe we were born and belong. So, whoever negatively discriminates a person because of his tribe is still in need of more enlightening. His action of discrimination is a clear indication of his ignorance. He does not know what he is doing.

What normally results in conflict amongst tribes is when a person brings in comparisons of value and quality; for example, arguing that tribe A is better than tribe B because of this or that. People who play these kinds of games show ignorance of what each tribe entails. Appreciating tribal features and characteristics can correct such wrong perceptions. So, instead of making tribes compete against or amongst themselves, encourage complementing one another while celebrating their differences.

3. Use Political Party affiliations as platform for dynamism

Political parties are legal forums or groups set with purpose to pursue recruitment of candidates for offices, run elections, set policies, provide leadership to the country and administrate the Nation. Political groups of kindred spirits seek to promote employment, fair distribution of national wealth, supervise environmental conservation and fight against human abuses as well as general crimes. In a nutshell, the purpose of forming political parties is to open a wider opportunity for displaying personal abilities by those who vie for national or State leadership. It is not for a means of creating enmity among political actors.

Political parties are supposed to be like football, boxing clubs and wrestling tags where the opponents work zealously hard during the game. They are emotionally charged with determination to win, celebrate and take metals and trophies. But at the end of the match or game, those opponents are friends; they shake hands and even congratulate the winner of the match.

Unfortunately, our political parties have become divisive, source of hatred and enmity.

> A person is a citizen in South Sudan not because of his political party affiliation.

Consequently, several prominent leaders have been killed by their rivals. The manner in which we treat political parties has caused untold suffering for citizens than good.

As it is in our countries today, we can confidently say these political parties do not add any value to our citizenship, nor do they bring change to human dignity. They are not important whether they exist or not. Reality reveals to us that actually we are very comfortable to live without them than having them. Unless we change our ideology from negativity to positivity and if they are formed, they must exist to facilitate a means to national leadership and to create opportunities for several people to participate in the exercise of politics and vying for such national leadership.

Political parties do not provide citizens with any identity. No, never! Hence, political parties should not be used to divide or cause hatred among the people. They should not be used for discrimination or job recruitment. Since they are just platforms, we as citizens should embrace them as means for displaying our leadership abilities only.

To accommodate is to accept someone as he or she is, despite their background, opinion or other affiliation. The Apostle Paul mentioned several things we need to practice in order to make this happen. They are discussed below:

1. Bearing with one another

To bear with is to tolerate, persevere or show patience in the face of suffering. It is a positive attitude towards an object that inflicts pain onto you. Let me put it this way, as we all know that in any family, the number of family member normally begins from two and more. Now every person in any family is different in behavior, with varied likes and dislikes. What you like may be what your spouse or child dislikes. In a similar way, what they like is not what you like. But because you are members of the same family, you must be patient with each other to maintain cohesion in the family.

Therefore, true family love calls for forbearing, tolerance and patience. For this to be effective there must be constant dialog whenever conflict arises. It is perhaps summed up by forgiveness.

2. Forgiving one another

Jack Kornfield, the renowned psychologist and teacher of Buddhist psychology, illustrates forgiveness with this story of a woman, her child and a young boy who killed the woman's only child.

> Therefore, true family love calls for forbearing, tolerance and patience.

Here the story goes: 'On the train from Washington to Philadelphia, while on my way to my father's memorial funeral service, I sat down next to an interesting fellow who worked with young boys, particularly those in jail and prison, as part of an inner-city project in Washington, DC. He told me this story'.

'A young kid, 14 years old, wanted to get into a gang. The way that he proved himself to enter the gang was to shoot somebody — it was an initiation rite. He shot this kid he didn't know. He was apprehended, brought to trial, and at the end of the trial, convicted'.

'Just before he is taken away in handcuffs, the mother of the boy who was shot stands up, looks him in the eye, and says, "I'm going to kill you," and then sits down. After being in prison for a year or so, the boy is visited by that mother, and he's kind of frightened. She says, "I've just got to talk with you." They have a little bit of conversation, and as she leaves him she says, "Do you need anything?

Cigarettes?" and she leaves him a little money'.

'She starts to visit him. She goes every few months, and over the course of three or four years, she starts visiting him more regularly, talking to him. When he's about to get out at the age of 17 or 18, she asks, "What are you going to do?" and he says, "I have no idea. I got no family, no nothing." And she says, "well I've got a friend who has a little factory—maybe I can help you get a job'."

'So she arranges that with the parole officer. Then she asks, "Where are you going to stay?" and he says, "I don't know where I'm going to go." And she says, "Well I have a spare room where you can stay with me." So he comes and stays in the spare room, takes this job, and after about six months, she says, "I really need to talk with you—come into the living room. Sit down, let's talk."

She looks at him and says, "Remember that day in court when you were convicted of murdering my son for no reason at all, to get into your gang, and I stood up and said, 'I'm going to kill you?'"

"Yes ma'am, I'll never forget that day," he says'.

'And she looks back and says, "Well, I have. You see, I didn't want a boy who could kill in cold blood like that to continue to exist in this world. So I set about visiting you, bringing you presents, bringing you things, and taking care of you. And now I let you come into my house and got you a job and a place to live because I don't have anybody anymore. My son is gone and he was the only person that I was living with. I set about changing you, and you're not that same person anymore. But I don't have anybody, and I want to know if you'd stay here. I'm in need of a son, and I want to know if I can adopt you." And he said yes and she did adopt him'.

From this story, we can say that forgiveness is that human capacity for considering another person's dignity no matter what the circumstances of life for that individual are. As the story shows, forgiveness is not just about the other. It's really for the beauty of your own soul. It is for your own capacity to fulfill your life.

Forgiveness is in particular, the capacity to let go, to release the suffering, the sorrows, the burdens of the pains and betrayals of the past, and instead to choose the mystery of love. Forgiveness shifts us from the small separate sense of ourselves to a capacity to renew, to let go, to live in love. If you want to see the brave, look to those who can return love for hatred. If you want to see the heroic, look to those who can forgive. Actually beating and killing another person for slapping or insulting you is being cowardly. A strong person forgives the wrong another person does to him, especially a person deemed to be weak one.

With forgiveness, we are unwilling to attack or wish harm on anyone, including ourselves. And without forgiveness, life would be unbearable. It's hard to imagine a world without forgiveness, because we would be chained to the suffering of the past and have only to repeat it over and over again. There would be no release. So it is not easy. Note that love and forgiveness are not for the faint-hearted, but for those who can bravely say, "It stops with me. I will not pass on to my children this sorrow. I will accept the betrayal and the suffering, and I will bare it, but I will not retaliate. I will not pass this onto the next generation, and to endless generations of grandchildren."

Psychologists generally look at forgiveness as "a conscious and deliberate decision to release feelings of resentment." When you release the wrong doer from the wrong, you cut a malignant tumor out of your inner life. You set a prisoner free, but you discover that the prisoner was yourself.

Fr. C. S. Drago, SJ emphasizes that forgiveness needs to be deemed as the noblest virtue of a man. In which, it springs from the deepest desire of our heart to be at peace with others (17, 18). You may know in the scripture that the Lord Jesus gave a command to all His followers to forgive their offenders and enemies.

Jesus Christ once says, *"If you forgive men when they sin against you, your heavenly Father will also forgive you. But if you do not forgive men their sins, your Father will not forgive your sins"* (NIV, Matthew 6.14-15). According to Jesus forgiveness stands in the very heart of human relationship with God. It is the factor that determines the degree of a persons' relation to God. Morley also says, "Our relationship with God depends on our willingness to forgive those who sin against us" (295). The model for human forgiveness is the forgiveness of God; humanity is called to forgive unconditionally as God does.

The fact of human freedom to choose whether to forgive or not is part of the fabric for human relations and co-existence in every society. Its practice demonstrates the true human nature and a person's distinctiveness as a being created in the true image of God. Humanity is unlike other created beasts that tear each other apart [add comma] because at one side of his center is an outpouring of mercy and love for even the unlovable human being. This is an incredible virtue that no other creature possesses. It is this that demonstrates human superiority over other beings.

How do we forgive?

We need to have a vision for forgiveness

Every human being is created to be in communion with God. A human being is designed for Union, Unity and Peace. Human attitudes, words and actions are supposed to be geared to enforcing union, unity and peace. The apostle Paul says, *"I urge you, brothers, to watch out for those who cause divisions and put obstacles in your way that are contrary to the teaching you have learned. Keep away from them. For such people are not serving Jesus Christ but their appetites"* (NIV, Romans 16.17-18). Forgiveness is one of the most important ministries any human being is expected to perform towards another. It is very relevant to the war-torn nation of South Sudan.

We need to set a pace for Forgiveness

On Thursday, 14th December 2016, the Sudan Tribune, a non-profit website, reports:

Addressing members of South Sudan's national legislative assembly in the capital Juba on Wednesday, President Kiir asked for forgiveness for the wrongs committed. He called for National dialogue, saying; "…in my view, national dialogue is both a forum and process through which the people of South Sudan can gather to redefine the basis of their unity as it relates to nationhood, and sense of belonging." The South Sudanese leader told the country's lawmakers. "In the light of national endeavor, I am calling upon all of you to forgive one another, enter into dialogue with one another at your personal capacities, and embrace yourselves," he said. In addition, he said, "I am asking you, the people of

South Sudan to forgive me for any wrong I might have committed."

The president's reported speech was an expression that can provide us with desires through which the act of genuine forgiveness can be obtained. His call to every South Sudanese will be the commitment to a process of true change in the young nation, but only if we so desire.

Nevertheless, the reality in South Sudan is that genuine forgiveness will only come when every hurting South Sudanese resolves personally to let go of the long-held resentments against one another. Where there is no forgiveness, the hurt someone inflicted on another will always remain. On the contrary, where genuine forgiveness takes place, that hurt is lessened because forgiveness diminishes its grip in the person's life.

We need to emphasize the necessity of forgiveness

The Apostle John writes to his audience saying,

"If we claim to be without sin, we deceive ourselves and the truth is not in us…and his word has no place in our lives. But if we confess our sins, he is faithful and just and he will forgive us our sins and purify us from all unrighteousness" (NIV, 1John1.8, 9).

In South Sudan, if both national leaders and citizens are frank with one another, their confession frees them to enjoy fellowship with Christ and with one another. It should ease the people's consciences and lighten their cares. God has impacted every South Sudanese with free will. The free will is each person's ability to decide and act freely, despite God's view and that of other people. A person is only in charge of himself in the exercise of free will. If a person refuses to forgive another person, nothing can force him to forgive. Yet, one must note that, he himself also needs others to forgive him when he does wrong to them. That is why forgiveness is God's gift, commanded to strengthen human relationships with one another, as it does our relationship with God.

Genuine forgiveness leads to feelings of understanding, empathy and compassion for the offender. This does not mean that you the hurting person ignore the offender's responsibility for hurting you. No, it simply implies that you the offended person forgives your offender as you personally decided to do. And it is a sign of complying with God's word. You are not forced to forgive but willingly do it because you have seen the   need for peace between you and them. Therefore, for you to forgive:

1) Choose   to do it without self-justification
2) Decide firmly not to be reverted

3) Think of the good it will bring between you two and other friends
4) Embrace attitude of humility, that is to consider others better than yourself

What is Humility?

Humility or humbleness is a state of a person's attitude whereby the person is meek or has an unassuming nature. Using the Apostle Paul's terms, humility can be described as *"honoring one another above oneself…Or not being proud or conceited"* (NIV, Romans 12: 9-16). Humility demands that we think of ourselves less than we think about others.   It manifests itself in our relationship with God and with others. We are to be humble toward God and His word, humble in regard to trials and blessings that come our way or abilities and achievements with which we are blessed and humble toward other people. So, humility is the proper attitude with which we serve our people (Bridges, 2001, 74).

A humble person treats people equally when he is in public office and he will accept public criticisms even if they are negative. The opposite of humility is PRIDE. Unfortunately, many people prefer to be proud when they achieve certain status in society. But little did they know that, in the book of Proverbs, God hates pride. As the Bible says, *"There are six things the LORD hates…haughty eyes, a lying tongue, hands that shed innocent blood, a heart that devises wicked schemes, feet that are quick to rush into evil, a false witness who pours out lies and a man who stirs up dissension among brothers"* (NIV, Proverbs 6:16-19).

How then can a person become humble?

We need to think right and good thoughts (Philippians 4:8-9)

This is thinking about yourself in comparison to others, but in a positive way; that you are not better than them but equal to them, or even better, that others are better than you.

This is important because many a time what makes a person proud is: education, wealth, size, color, and tribal population. Right thinking tells you that having those assets and numbers do not affect your true humanness. Your value and dignity as a human being still remains the same. You don't become super human because you are rich, powerful and born in a large tribe. If you think like that, then you are deceiving yourself. The important thing in life is relationship with God and with other people because when you die, you will need people to bury your body here in the soil, not in the air. Knowing these realities should be enough to humble us.

We need to Accept Criticism from others

Criticism is the practice of judging the merits and faults of someone. As an evaluative or corrective exercise, criticism can occur in any area of human life. Therefore, criticism takes many different forms. How people go about in responding to those criticisms can also vary a great deal. It is the aspect of response that demonstrates your true nature or character. For example, if people negatively criticize you and your work, do you react angrily or you take it cool. To take it cool is possible and the best because you would avoid conflicts with others and hurting yourself by harboring bad thoughts.

You probably are aware that all decisions of doing wrong or bad and that of doing right and good all depends on you. Nobody can force you to fight or even kill you, when you choose not to do it. Do not be misled that when you fight a person for abusing you, you shall be free from your actions. Infect, you are guilty for boxing, beating or slapping the other person. So, always put your emotions down when provoked by another person; think through before you act.

We need to stop the tradition of Revenge

What have you ever gained by revenging, if indeed you have done it? Suppose you have retaliated back at somebody by killing the person that killed your relative, has it brought back your dead relative? Have you added more friends or won that person's relatives over to your support? No, it normally create more enemies for you, so the best way is [add `to'] love.

What is revenge then?

Revenge is vengeance and vengeance is retaliation and retaliation is reprisal and reprisal is doing a bad thing to a person because he first did badly to you. Jesus once taught that, we must stop doing such kind of things to our fellow human beings. He says, *"You have heard that it was said, "love your neighbor and hate your enemy. But I tell you: Love your enemies and pray for those who persecute you, that you may be sons of your Father in heaven. He causes his sun rise on the evil and the good, and sends rain on the righteous and the unrighteous"* (NIV, Matthew 5:38-45).

The Apostle Paul restated this teaching in the book of Romans, saying *"Do not repay anyone evil for evil … It is mine to avenge; I will repay … On contrary: if your enemy is hungry, feed him; if he is thirsty, give him something to drink … Do not be overcome by evil, but overcome evil with good"* (NIV, Romans 12:17-21).

Many a times in self deceit we think revenge or paying back evil with evil can solve our problem. Little did we know that by revenging, we are multiplying the number of our enemies? We need to understand that each time we kill a person because he is an enemy, we create more enemies. Why, because all the relatives, friends and sympathizers join to fight against us who revenged. The unfortunate thing is most of us do not know this truth, so we keep on doing revenging on people we deemed to be our enemies.

But the way to conquer our enemy is by emulating or practicing the principle of our Lord, Jesus Christ. Look! How He treated those accused and killed Him; instead of hate, He loved them. He forgave them and by doing so He conquered not only His enemies but the greater number from the human race.

Today, millions of people including you perhaps and me willingly come to follow Him.

We need to understand that each time we kill a person because he is an enemy, we create more enemies.

Remember –
love is the most excellent way.

Use it. Love is the sure method for quenching flames of bitterness and hatred.

For you to learn this, put it into practice. Today, if you meet a person on the way, greet the person with a smile. You will be surprised that the person you greeted with a smile will also greet you back with a smile on his face.

After trying the way of love, change, and try the way of anger and hate instead. Meet a person, be angry at him and insult that person straight away. As you did to him, he will do to you. And you will become or remain enemies. This routine life-cycle of relationship controls us daily. Nevertheless, you do have the mantle under your control. As a family of one nation, we need to put our love in action by expressing it through sharing and caring for one another, for everyone.

Let me say in a positive way, that the good things that originate in a family are enormous. Those things that amuse, excite and make people happy also come from good families. So how can we accept our differences?

We can accept differences in the family by learning and practicing the importance of unity.

In a family, we are all different; each family member has his own likes and dislikes.

Love covers multitudes of wrongs. The word the Apostle Paul uses in managing living together is to "bear" and "bear with one another". This word could be reiterated as, 'tolerate' or 'endurance'. In a family, we are all different; each family member has his own likes and dislikes. These likes and dislikes are not only with one person but with every member of the family. As you bear with me, you are not doing me favor. No, you need to understand that I am also bearing with your bad manners. As you bear with me, I also do with you – none of us is absolutely perfect. Do not deceive yourself that your conducts and behaviors are better than mine, there is nothing like that.

When I keep quiet with your odd behaviors, I should not think it is only you who has that bad behavior, because I also have bad behaviors too. The suffering you are causing me is similar to the suffering I am causing you. None of us is better by far in any way than the other. That is why Jesus said, no one is 'perfect' except God alone...and that before I point out the small speck in your eyes, I must first remove the big log in my eyes (NIV, Matthew 7:1-5). If I know these truths, and you know them also, then we shall be able to bear, respect and love one another.

*"And now I will show you the most
excellent way"* (NIV, 1 Corinthians 13:1),
writes the Apostle Paul.

What is the most excellent way? The
most excellent way is the way of love.
*"… Love each other deeply, because love
covers over multitude of sins"* (NIV, 1
Peter 4:8) writes the Apostle Peter. With
genuine love all around, no person in
our nation will ever feel rejection,
isolation or banished. It is only in the
world of love that we can unfold and
blossom. With love, our nation becomes
a circle of unity, strength and home as
one big family. Love must be sincere
and must not keep records of wrongs,
cries the Apostle Paul.

What is love?

Love is an emotional drive and affection towards another person with the purpose of good will towards them.

There are three types of love but the love we need in family and our nation of South Sudan is what I call here 'superior or perfect love.'

> It is only in the world of love that we can unfold and blossom.

Superior love is also known as perfect love. It bears this name because it is the Love of God. According to Apostle John, *"God is love and perfect love comes from Him only"* (NIV, 1 John 4:8). Regarding this perfect love, the Apostle John states: *"There is no fear in love … because perfect love drives out fear."* Fear has to do with wrong actions that deserve punishment by law enforcers.

Our responsibility as citizens of one nation, therefore, is to love one another in this godly way. We should not be like Cain, who was evil in that he murdered his own brother. Some of us know the story of Cain and his younger brother, Abel. Both were the children of Adam, the first man God created. The two sons had different careers. Cain was a farmer, while his follower Abel was a shepherd. One day, Cain told his brother Abel to go with him to a lonely place where they could offer sacrifices to God. Abel accepted, so they went. While in the field Cain attacked his younger brother Abel and killed him. The reason that made Cain kill his brother was jealousy. Abel's prayer and offerings were received by God, while God refused the offerings of Cain, because Cain had wrong motives, which God warned him about. God wanted Cain to repent from his wrong motive but Cain didn't repent. The result was murder. The Bible therefore, warns us not to follow in the footsteps of Cain, the killer of his own brother.

The lesson for us here is not to do things with wrong motives, nor to kill our fellow citizens. The Bible treats the heart attitude as a serious matter, saying, *"…anyone who hates his brother is a murderer … and anyone who does not love his brother whom he has seen, cannot love God, whom he has not seen* (NIV, 1 John 3:11, 12, 15). That is how serious it is to God. We can't say we love God if we have hatred towards a brother or a sister. We are called upon to be sincere from heart, in attitude, and by volition.

In the book of Corinthians, the Apostle Paul approved love to be the most excellent way for every acceptable action as this sub-section has discussed above. This means that we must embrace love to guide all our decisions and actions. Any action that is prompted by love is blameless and upright. Perfect love can be distinguished from other types of love because love:

1. Cares

To care is to be thoughtful, considerate, compassionate, gentle and self dedication. All of us one time experienced and enjoyed caring from our mothers at the time of infancy. What I am saying here is when God gives you responsibility of leadership; you need to exhibit this attitude towards your people. Identify with people in any of their situation, this is being human and bearing mothers' heart.

Every human being needs care, whether they are great, educated, and rich. Without a selfless attitude of caring for one another, the family and society will never experience peace. On caring, Apostle Paul says, *"Each of you should look not only to your own interests, but also to the interest of others"* (NIV, Philippians 2:4). And James adds by asking:

What good is it, my brothers, if a man claims to have faith but has no deeds? ... Suppose a brother or sister is without clothes and daily food. If one of you says to him, 'Go I wish you well, keep warm and well fed', but does nothing about his physical needs, what good is it? In the same way, faith by itself, if not accompanied by action is dead ... do you not know that, religion that God our Father accepts as pure and faultless is this: to look after orphans and widows in their distress and to keep oneself from being polluted by the world. (NIV, James 1:27; 2:14-17).

Proverbs also says, *"If a man shuts his ears from the cry of the poor, he too will cry out and not be answered"* (NIV, Proverbs 21:13). All these scriptural texts teach us about sharing as a sign of true love.

2. Is sincere

Sincerity is an act of being open, frank and honesty. In our society, many people don't practice sincerity. People like hiding away from being truthful. Every time people prefer to lying, and cheating instead of truthfulness. Consequently, in our families, children learn to lie and cheat at the tender ages. The more we practice this culture, the more we promote the work of the devil in our homes, communities and society. Doing that shows that we don't love one another and don't care too.

3. It Shares

Perfect love shares. And sharing is an act of willingness to apportion and distribute personal, public and ancestral resources with "family" members. In a broader sense, sharing is generosity which negatively is seen in greed, selfishness, and parsimony.

One vital quality of generosity, also known as munificence, is free-will giving. Munificence normally aims at supporting destitute people in their misery. On the contrary, sharing is an obligation towards other people regardless of their family background, social and political status, as well as their gender and age. Let me illustrate this with this brief story:

In those days, hunting for food was a popular social activity such as sports. Two or more villages would come together, select their finest huntsmen and send them on a hunting expedition deep into the woods. Two of my elder brothers and some of my cousins, more often than not were chosen to represent our village. If they were fortunate enough to kill an animal, let's say the animal is a good size deer, it was normal that the meat must be shared across the entire family.

It happened that my father had two brothers and these uncles of mine also had their own families. So, when my eldest brother killed the deer, he sent a message to my eldest cousins in the families of my both uncles offering to give them each pieces of the meat. If it was my second eldest brother, he would correspond with my second eldest cousins, and the pattern goes on.

Furthermore, after finishing the distribution in your father's family and relatives, you are also required to share the meat with the people who went hunting with you.

Hence, the idea of sharing in the family is an old concept, which has been passed from generation to generation.

This is done until you, the owner of the carcass, remains only with the head of the animal. Wow! Nevertheless, you feel great because it is an honor to be crowned by elders and family members as the best hunter. So, you enjoy the glory of sharing joyously, forgetting the small quantity of meat you are left with.

Hence, the idea of sharing in the family is an old concept, which has been passed from generation to generation. Family resources belong to every member of the family. It does not matter whether the resources are acquired by an individual family member or inherited from fore parents.

What is the importance of sharing?

- It promotes unity
- It eradicates poverty among people
- It opens wide opportunities to earn more resources

How does sharing open opportunities?

Sharing invokes God's blessings because God values sharing. In the book of Timothy, Apostle Paul admonished Timothy to instruct people to share their resources with one another. *"Command them ... "to do good, to be rich in good deeds, and to be generous and willing to share"* (NIV, 1 Timothy 6:18-19). He says this is because sharing has an eternal value and it lays a foundation for the life to come.

Which resources do we need to share?

Human Resources

In South Sudan, as it is in other countries, one outstanding wealth of the country is its human resources. People are the heritage of the land on which they live. Take human beings away from any land they live on and that land has no meaning: it cannot develop and cannot be called a nation by itself. Unfortunately, we in South Sudan just like many other African countries still regard human beings as second hand resource: we kill them for the sake of attaining power, cattle, land, money and oil. Why do we do this?

Let us know that the people who come from the sixty-four tribes of South Sudan are the combined human resources of the country. Just look at the key factors concerning human beings:

The value and dignity of human beings are higher than any other created thing here on earth, so they cannot be compared to any [add `other'] non-human resource.

The fact is that human beings are highly dignified and must not be treated lightly.

Destroy human resources and you have destroyed the nation.

They are all equal to each other. None are like other created things, especially animals.

Human dignity is God imparted and does not need to be measured by the level of education or socio-economic status and tribal prejudice.

The worth of human beings deserves respect, love and fair treatment.

This point emphasizes the earlier statement that human resource is the greatest resource as compared to other resources in the country of South Sudan. This is because human beings are created in the image of God. If there is no human resource in a nation, then that nation CANNOT develop. Destroy human resources and you have destroyed the nation. IT IS NO MORE.

Human resources call for understanding of all people's talents and gifting. For a country like South Sudan to develop faster, its leadership needs to set their minds to discovering and understanding people's talents, skills and gifting.

How do you do this?

You can do it in two forums, home and school. Once the abilities of every individual South Sudanese is known and understood, they should be assigned to various jobs appropriately. To do this effectively, the leaders must throw away the practice of nepotism. If your brother, sister, wife/husband, son or nephew is not qualified for any job, do not give him the job. Designate people to various jobs based on merit, if we do this, I promise you that the outcome will be incredible.

Human resources need to be shared widely in the country

Currently in South Sudan, some states and their counties have less skilled and educated people. This must call for more human resource from others alike. A State or county with more qualified manpower needs to share with the starving states and counties. A nation as a family must embrace the fact of allowing every South Sudanese to work and live anywhere in our land of South Sudan.

There is a distinct need to avoid persecuting fellow South Sudanese citizens from another ethnic group for working or settling among a different ethnic group. Let me put this in a question form: Suppose your land is stricken by a disaster, like drought and famine, will you not accept any food and money from the other ethnic groups as relief?

If you can accept the food or money of another South Sudanese who does not belong to your tribe, why then do you refuse to allow him work in your area?

Hating me for being in another tribe means you are waging war against God for creating other tribes in South Sudan.

Why do you hate me and want to kill me because I am a Madi? Did I apply to God to be born in Madi tribe?

Listen to what the Bible says, *"Do not mistreat an alien or oppress him..."* (Exodus 22:21). Instead welcome strangers (aliens) in your home, county and State. (Hebrews 13:2). This is because a foreigner who settles or works in your Payam or county brings with him God's blessings. We have seen earlier that it is God who determines where people must live. When God decides that people from different areas come to settle and work in your native land, do not resist them but welcome them as brothers and sisters.

Our Native Land

Another important resource of South Sudan is its land. Land is a native soil where every tribe is settled as determined by God from the beginning (NIV, Acts 17:26). By birth, a person qualifies to occupy his ancestral area. But that's not all. People are also allowed to buy extra land in different locations in the Republic of South Sudan. Therefore, people need not to be confined on their ancestral heritages only but be able to buy land and settle anywhere in the country. This however must not be a one sided exchange where by other tribes can come by force or peacefully settle on other people's ancestral areas but the same tribe would not allow some tribes to settle in their area. Let us have concern for each other, if you would like to settle in my tribal land, then you should also allow my tribesman to settle in your ancestral land.

Apart from individual citizens owning land for their own use, the government demarcates certain portions of land for its operations. Where land becomes a government property and it wishes to sell to private investment or individuals, the leaders need to uphold fairness to avoid conflicts. In any society where justice governs in administration, peace will prevail. But if justice is thrown out from the law, land-wrangling issues will begin to prevail. Once that happens, our country will lose a lot of precious resources in trying to resolve numerous land disputes.

To administer justice during land allocations, people need to:

- Recognize the right of every South Sudanese individual.
- Promote equality for all South Sudanese as members of just one family.
- Be content with their own share because greed is destructive.

The natural and non-natural Resources

These other resources include: water bodies, fish, wild animals, forests, oil reserves, sand, grass, mountains/rocks and stones. These resources are scattered all over the country. Some areas have plenty of rocks/stones while others have oil reserves, others have forests for wood and timber, and still others have water bodies for fish and so forth.

So, how should these resources is shared in our country? I'll answer this question with a story that is in the Bible. The story goes like this:

Once upon a time, the nation of Israel had conflict with Aram, a neighboring nation. Ben-Hadad the King of Aram marched against Israel and besieged it. In ancient times, cities were fenced with thick walls for protection purposes. The Israelites also fenced their city, Jerusalem, so that the Aramean army could not break into the city and kill people. As a result the Arameans surrounded the city of Jerusalem to prevent the Israelites from coming out.

All the Israelites were trapped inside the walls of the city; they could not come out to engage the Aramean soldiers in battle due to fear. The siege took many months, such that all the food stuff in the city was finished. When food was not available for the people to eat, two women agreed to eat their children. The first woman killed her son, cooked him and they ate him. The following day, the woman whose child was eaten on the previous day said to her colleague, *"today is your turn, bring your son, we cook him and eat him."* But then the woman hid her child, so that the second woman's son was not eaten. This made the woman whose child was eaten seek for justice from the king who was passing by her area.

After the woman whose son was eaten realized that she was tricked by her friend, she became sorrowful and sad. With much sorrow and sadness, she went with the matter to the king of Israel and narrated the story to him as the king listened intently. After hearing the sad story, the king was enraged, and tore his clothes in anger.

As we all know, when disaster comes upon a nation or an individual, people would always want to find the cause of it. So, the king's point of view was that, the disaster was caused by God. The prophet of God Elisha was nearby. The king sent his messenger with one of the leading army commanders to kill the prophet Elisha.

Before they could arrive, Elisha already knew from God that the king was sending somebody to kill him. He told his elders *"Don't you see this murderer is sending someone to cut off my head? Look here the messenger comes. Shut the door and hold it shut against him. Is this not the sound of his master's footsteps behind him?"*

Before long, the messenger arrived, as the prophet Elisha was about to talk. The king also arrived and said to the prophet, "This disaster is from the LORD. Why should I wait for the LORD any longer?" To that, Elisha replied, *"Hear the word of the LORD. This is what the LORD says: About this time tomorrow, a seah of flour will sell for a shekel and two seahs of barley for shekel at the gate of Samaria."* The following day, what the prophet said happened exactly as he had told the king of Israel.

But how did this happen?

The Bible tells us: The Lord God caused the Arameans to hear the sounds of chariots and horses, a great army coming to attack their camp. This caused fear in them, so they said to one another, *"Look the king of Israel has hired the Hittite and Egyptian kings to attack us!"* So they got up and fled in the dust abandoning their tents and their horses and their donkeys. They left their camp just as it was and ran for their lives.

How did the Israelites know that the Arameans had fled?

The report was brought by four lepers. The story says that there were four men who had contagious leprosy on their bodies. They were staying at the gate of the city inside the fence. The men discussed among themselves and agreed to go to the Arameans and ask for food. They said to themselves, "If the Arameans welcome us, well and good.

In case the Aramean army kills us, still no problem. After all, we are going to die soon because of this famine." So they went and reached the camp only to discover the Aramean army was no longer there. They had fled and left all their properties behind.

The men entered in one of the tents where they found food, gold, silver and some drink, which they ate and drank. They carried away silver, gold and clothes, and went off to hide them. Then they returned and entered another tent, took some more things from it and hid them also. Then they said to each other, *"we're not doing right. This is a day of good news and we are keeping it to ourselves. If we wait until daylight, punishment will overtake us. Let's go at once and report this to the royal palace..."*

The Bible story you have just read teaches everyone lessons on how to share national resources amongst fellow citizens.

How do we share national resources?

We need to be conscious in doing right!

To be conscious is a sense of self awareness and responsibility towards others. People with high sensitivity to self are those who keenly observe their beliefs, moral values and societal norms. These are people of integrity, in the sense that they know what they believe, and what they say in words and actions. They are accountable in all that they do and execute their roles towards others as it is expected of them.

The four men with leprosy are portrayed as this kind of citizens, those who know what they believed and what their responsibilities were towards their fellow citizens. They talked among themselves and decided, *"We are not doing right..."* What was it that they were not doing right? It was their act of hiding resources for themselves while others in the city were starving. What resource do you have in your possession, or in your native land, that you do not want to share with other tribes of the family of South Sudan? What is it that you hide from other citizens, in the far away banks of other nations? Do you feel guilty or not?

We need to take the good news to others.

Disclosing to others what you could call personal luck shows a sense of selflessness. You are renouncing and detaching yourself from greed. This is a high virtue obtained from God alone. To do that, you need to tell yourself, *"This is a day of good news and we are keeping it to ourselves."* We should not keep good news of things that can revive our nation to ourselves. Let us learn from these four untouchable men to do what is right.

We need to be Retributive

Retribution is act of paying back to someone according to his just deserts.

Retribution usually happens to balance the

injustice someone has done to another although not exclusively considered in terms of punishment for wrongdoing. It distinctively talks about God's remunerative justice by distributing rewards to the obedient and His retributive justice in expressing His wrath against sin by inflicting penalties on the disobedient (NIV, Revelation 20.12b, 13).

According to the Bible Gateway Encyclopedia, the source of retribution is the nature of God. The doctrine of retribution flows from the very nature of God. The God of Scripture is a God clearly characterized by righteousness, justice, and omnipotence.   He can punish every evil and reward all righteousness. Though God is merciful and loving, nevertheless, God does not ignore evil. Rather He will punish evil people according to what their deeds deserve.

In the Bible, the book of 2 Chronicles tells us a story of war between the two kingdoms of Israel. The kingdom in the north went and attacked the kingdom of the south and defeated them severely. The soldiers of the northern kingdom killed those people in the southern kingdom without mercy, plundered their resources and carried some of them off as slaves. Remember, these are all people originally from the same kingdom that became divided. So, when the soldiers arrived with the captives from the southern kingdom chained and naked, the elders and the political leaders were not happy with the soldiers, wondering how the soldiers could mistreat their own brothers in that manner. Hence, the elders confronted their own soldiers and ordered them to return the captives they had captured to Jerusalem. The soldiers had to obey the orders of their leaders and returned the people with their properties back to Judah. In the process, they treated the sick, clothed the naked, and carried the weak on their own donkeys, back to Jerusalem ((NIV, 2 Chronicles 28.14). This text teaches South Sudanese people to do the same in our country today in order to end the raging war. Let us know that retribution by God is:

Why do we need retribution?

It is Inevitable

Biblical retribution is inevitable as pictured in various Bible books. In Galatians, the Apostle Paul strongly warns, *"Do not be deceived; God is not mocked, for whatever a man sows, that he will also reap. For he who sows to his own flesh will from the flesh reap corruption; but he who sows to the Spirit will from the Spirit reap eternal life."* (NIV, Galatians 6.7, 8). This is not the only reflection on retribution. Others are found in Old Testament books, for example: *"You have plowed iniquity, you have reaped injustice"* (NIV, Hosea 10:13) says the prophet Hosea. The use of this parable of the sowing seed indicates that punishment is an inner necessity and a natural consequence. But ONLY punishment by the right authorities

It is suitable to punish law breakers

The Bible stresses that there is a "poetic justice," a punishment which exactly fits the crime. As Jesus taught, *"For with the judgment you pronounce you will be judged also and the measure you give will be the same measure you will get"* (NIV, Matthew 7.2). The writer of the book of Proverbs states: that *"He who digs a pit will fall into it and a stone will come back upon him who starts its rolling"* (NIV, Proverbs 26.27). And in Revelation, it says, *"For men have shed the blood of saints and prophets, and you have given them blood to drink. It is their due!"* (NIV, Revelation 18:6, 7).

It is for current life and the future

The Old Testament books emphasize retribution in this life as recorded in the book of Psalms and it is also mentioned in many other passages such as Proverbs (NIV, Psalms 1.1; Proverbs 11.31). This simply means that, true justice is implied in an unjust society, when the perpetrators of such a cataclysm are squarely punished for their actions. Then the sufferers of mistreatment in the past wars of South Sudan will be fairly compensated. It is vital to note that God uses human instruments to carry out His retribution (Bible Gateway Encyclopedia). A clear example is when He used the Babylon kingdom to punish wicked Judah (NIV,

Habakkuk 1.6). This means, South Sudan can set up some customary judicial processes to arbitrate criminal cases. The book of Nehemiah sets a practical example here for the South Sudanese to emulate. In his time, those who felt mistreated, robbed of their properties such as land, unpaid salaries and wages were retrieved. Here goes the biblical narrative:

"Now the men and their wives raised a great outcry against their Jewish brothers. Some were saying, "We and our sons and daughters are numerous; in order for us to eat and stay alive, we must get grain." Others were saying, "We are mortgaging our fields, our vine yards and our homes to get grain during the famine." Still others were saying, we have had to borrow money to pay the king's tax on our fields and vine yards. Although we are of the same flesh and blood as our countrymen and though our sons are as good as theirs, yet we have to subject our sons and daughters to slavery. Some of our daughters have already been enslaved, but we are powerless, because our fields and vine yards belong to others ... when I heard their outcry and these charges, I was very angry ... so I called together a large meeting to deal with them and said: "As far as possible, we have bought back our Jewish brothers who were sold to Gentiles". Now you are selling your brothers ... what you are doing is not right ... so give back to them immediately their fields, vine yards, olive groves, houses, and also the usury you are charging them the hundredth part of the money, grains, new wine and oil (NIV, Nehemiah 5.1-11)

Over the past years of civil strife in South Sudan, similar things have happened to local people of the young nation. There is an outcry of indiscriminative killing all over the country. There are stories of looting, raping, unpaid salaries & wages, and land grabbing, false law suits and some undeserved charges, forcibly paid by people who are in weak positions. Those ill mistreatments were carried out by fellow South Sudanese against their own family, South Sudanese people. Henceforth, restitution is the only answer to avert all that has happened. As Nehemiah told the Jewish nobles, *"… give back to them immediately their fields, vine yards, olive groves, houses and also the usury you are charging them, the hundredth part of the money, grains, new wine and oil."* This will be the only way forward to reconcile all with one another in South Sudan.

Reconciliation is a change in relationship between two hostile parties, which effectively takes place when the parties in contest humbly submit to each other's demands in a spirit of self-denial and sacrifice. In the Bible, reconciliation is a change of relationship between God and man. The reconciliation in this context comes to us through the redemptive work of Christ on the cross.

Biblically, reconciliation between God and man is made possible through the death of Christ. This means God considers the death of His Son providing expatiation for man's sins. Henceforth, the wrath of God has been turned away from sinful mankind enabling man's acceptance by God.

Applying the same concept to our situation in South Sudan, reconciliation targets the involved parties in the current conflict. It requires all the parties to renounce their hostilities, to humbly come together without pre-conditions, in the spirit of deep concern for the interests of the ordinary citizens of our young Country.

In 1999 an international meeting was held in England, in which 120 prominent participants from 50 countries gathered. It was discussed that a new approach for Penal Reforms needed to be done for a New Century. Reconciliation then was baptized with a new name, *"Alternative Dispute Resolution"* (Tartisio, 69).   Alternative Dispute Resolution provides options that take disputes out of the panel justice arena and help the parties to resolve their issues with the assistance of a neutral person, such as a mediator (Ibid, 69-70). The driving forces behind this aim is to allow each party an opportunity of freedom to give up their own rights for the sake of the other and of their ongoing relationship. This can be done in three levels, which are discussed below:

1. Inter-personal level

In this context, two warring parties: the Sudan People's Liberation Army-In Government (SPLA-IG) and Sudan People's Liberation Army-In Opposition (SPLA-IO) are to be brought together to openly talk to each other with honesty. Each party's wrongs must be mentioned without fear and shame. And no party is allowed to call for self-defense. And none should be offended when their wrongs are pointed out. Rather, every party must be expected to forsake or leave its own rights to re-establish a new relationship.

This principle is derived from God, when He demonstrated His love and justice to mankind by sending Jesus Christ to die for mankind's sin. God has shown the way, so let people be likeminded and follow Him. The Apostle Paul further observes, *"very rarely will anyone die for a righteous man ... but God demonstrates his own love for us in this: while we were still sinners, Christ died for us"* (NIV, Romans 5.7-8). Let us learn to die for our fellow citizens by doing right and good. I am not talking about defense of self-interests here but about always considering others better than ourselves.

Favorable condition

Reconciliation of conditions presents the opportunity for the new relationship to flourish in an environment that is fair for every party. In his second book to the church of Corinth, the Apostle Paul writes, *"...if anyone is in Christ, he is a new creation, the old has gone, and the new has come! All this is from God, who reconciled us to himself through Christ ... not counting men's sins against them"* (NIV, 2Corinthians 5.17, 18-19). Here lies the most important aspect of reconciliation. It calls people not to count their former enemies' sins against them.

Reconciliation is mostly difficult and almost impossible in South Sudan because people like paying back their enemies in the same way for the evil that was committed against them.

Allow people to express themselves freely as God had already given them that freedom.

NO, it must not be like that. Let forgiveness and desire for one another overrule the past. Allow people to express themselves freely as God had already given them that freedom. You see, God does not put 'police angels' to follow us everywhere we go, or to control our talks. Whether we are talking evil things against Him or not, He allows people their freedom. That is why every human being has a mouth for talking. True reconciliation calls for encouraging environments with good security.

2. Empathy level

Empathy is an understanding of the situation of a person who is suffering, so as to identify with them. The Christian golden rule says, *"…in everything do to others what you would have them do to you, for this sums up the Law and the Prophets"* (NIV, Matthew 7.12). This principle basically addresses the heart of human reconciliation, which is also known as the Alternative Dispute Resolution. The questions that arise are these, 'do you often justify and push the blame on to others? Or do you show mercy to whoever deserves (needs?) it'? Empathy is doing to that other person, what you would want him to do to you.

The fact of reconciliation comes when it flows from the intrinsic human heart, without any external force.

As Morley says, *"If we could read the secret history of our enemies, we should find in each man's life sorrow and suffering enough to disarm all hostility"* (Op cit 288). In other words, no one enjoys bad and spoiled relationships.

But reality tells us that everyone strives for restoration of relationships and fellowship.

If anybody does, then he should not be afraid of the police after he has committed a crime against another person. If people enjoy crime, they should not hide themselves after a crime is committed, nor try to deny the truth. But reality tells us that everyone strives for restoration of relationships and fellowship. But because a person can't create the right atmosphere for restoration, he keeps on doing wrong and escaping the situation. Let kindness reign. People need to emulate Christ. He came to give love and sacrifice His life for those who did not deserve it. As the Apostle John says, *"Greater love has no one than this, which he laid down his life for his friends"* (NIV, John 15.13).

3. Transformation Level

"…I urge you brothers, in view of God's mercy…be transformed by the renewing of your mind." says, the Apostle Paul (NIV, Romans 12.1-2). Biblical transformation is the act of God in changing man's sinful nature into holiness. The process begins at the dawn of regeneration, when a person accepts Jesus Christ into his life as Lord. It is this change that the Apostle Paul says, *"…if anyone is in Christ, he is a new creation; the old is gone, the new has come"* (NIV, 2 Corinthians 5.17). During transformation, the will of man is paramount, without which the Holy Spirit would not work effectively.

But with man's cooperation, the metamorphosis that occurs connects him to God, to himself and to the community he lives in.

In his writing, the Apostle Paul demands for transformation of the mind, attitudes and the heart.

Nevertheless, Luther's reforms didn't survive the test of time.

Transformation is not reformation as many would think.

According to MacMillan reformation is just improving something which has gone bad (608). But transformation is making something completely new, with totally different status (783).

In human history, many reforms have been carried out by different people. One of the outstanding reformations was that of Martin Luther. Dowley describes him as the greatest German reformer like no any other figure in history, except Christ (368). Nevertheless, Luther's reforms didn't survive the test of time. The corruption, sexual immorality, racism and other human abuses which he fought, are all back in the church today. Dowley again comments that, in the event, after all Martin Luther's reformation endeavors, the heart-condition of the Christian Church remained unreformed (352).

A similar scenario follows in politics. Many politicians have tried reforms in their political systems over the past generations. They fought wars to make things better, but all became null and void. This conveys a clear message that all those who take up arms in the name of bringing political reforms will never make it. Why? Because many people have attempted those things before but no long term good came of them. Their actions caused death to many people, properties got destroyed and developments were retarded while always hoping that better results would come. But even the 'better' they fought for, never lasted. That is why the Bible offers principles that deal with the transformation rather than reformation of the human mind, attitude and heart.

Transformation of the mind

The human mind is the center of contemplation, comprehension and resolution. It is the very element in a human being which differentiates him from other living creatures. There are three elements that form the human personality: the mind, the will, and the emotions. With the mind a man thinks, comprehends and make decisions on issues. Due to this, the Apostle Paul admonishes the Christians in Rome to, *"…be transformed by the renewing of your (their) mind"* (NIV, Romans 12.2). Why? Because the book of Proverbs says, *"for as he thinketh in his heart, so is he…"* (KJV, Proverbs 23.7b).

Tracy agrees with this concept, so he writes, ...the most important mental and spiritual principle ever discovered is that you become what you think about most of the time.

Your outer world is very much a mirror image of your inner world. What is going on outside of you reflects what is going on inside of you.

You can tell the inner condition of a person by looking at the outer conditions of his or her life. And it cannot be otherwise. (xiv).

Murphy echoed the same view, saying; *"... it is the world within, namely, your thoughts, feelings, and imagery, that makes your world without. It is therefore, the only creative power and everything which you find in your world of expression has been created by you in the inner world of your mind, either consciously or unconsciously"* (6, 7).

The emphasis here is that the mind plays a central part in man's actions. The mind is extraordinarily powerful. That is why a person's thoughts control and determine almost everything that happens to him. Thoughts can make a person happy or sad. Thoughts trigger images, pictures and the emotions that go with them. Then the images, pictures and emotions prompt attitudes and actions. The actions therefore, have consequences and results that determine what happens to the person (Ibid, xiv, xv). So, the Apostle is very particular on what part of human body deserves transformation. It is not the leg or the hands but the mind (NIV, Romans 12.2). To have a mind transformed means, emptying the mind from all wrong ideas of hatred and revenge, [add `and'] then refilling it with love for all people. Day by day, we must engage our minds with positive healthy thoughts. As the Apostle Paul demands, " ... *brothers, whatever is true, whatever is noble, whatever is right, whatever is pure, whatever is lovely, whatever is admirable – if anything is excellent or praiseworthy – think about such things*" (NIV, Philippians 4.8).

Transformation of the Attitude

"*...be made new in the attitude of your mind*" (NIV, Ephesians 4.23) "*Your attitude should be the same as that of Christ Jesus*" (NIV, Philippians 2.4-5).

An attitude is the mental state of a person, formed by his past and current experiences. (Wikipedia). Macmillan defines an attitude as, "an opinion or feeling that ... shows a person's behavior" (47). An attitude serves as a pair of glasses through which a person sees the world around him. Once a person has a formed attitude towards a person, it will always be expressed through words and other body languages.

In the Bible, there is a story of a man called Nathanael. One day, Philip met with Jesus and decided to become one of Jesus' disciples. So excited about his new relationship with Jesus, Philip invited Nathanael to join him in following Jesus. But Nathanael had an attitude towards people from Nazareth. When Philip told Nathaniel that Jesus was a man from Nazareth, Nathanael immediately asked Philip: *"Can anything good come out from there?"* (NIV, John 1.46). Nathanael's response was negative as far as anything had connections to Nazareth. To him, Nazarenes were underdogs. Nobody was capable of anything good. But his attitude was wrong.

Cultivating an attitude

An attitude develops when a person's well-being involves his [add `or her'] hormonal fluctuations due to changes in diet, family and community lifestyles. Both in the family and in community, a person acquires certain behavior patterns from the way other people practice their beliefs and values. In communities where moral and ethical standards are low, a person will develop negative attitudes towards people or other things.

How does one cultivate an attitude of anger and revenge?

Anger and revenge are negative human emotions that are dangerous to an individual and to the person towards who anger and revenge is built up. Revenge develops from unreleased anger towards someone or a group of people.

It results from an unforgiving heart, against which the Bible urges, *"Get rid of all bitterness, rage and anger, brawling and slander, along with every form of malice"* (NIV, Ephesians 4.31). The Bible commands, *"Do not repay anyone evil for evil … Do not take revenge … but leave room for God's wrath"* (NIV, Romans 12.17-19).

A negative attitude is destructive to an individual and to any other person towards whom the negative attitude is directed.

Transformation of the Heart

The word "heart" possesses nuances of centrality. It is used in Scriptures literally to refer to the inner most part of beings. In Hebraic thought, the heart is comprehensive in its operations as the seat of intellectual, affective, volitional and religious life … it is the main organ of the psychic center of human affections and the source of spiritual life (1-3).

Douglas has a similar description, saying the heart is essentially the whole man, with all his attributes, physical, and intellectual and psychological, of which the Hebrews thought and spoke, and the heart was conceived as the governing center for all of these. It is the heart that makes a man and governs all his actions (456).

Jesus affixed His affirmation to this fact in the gospel of Matthew, "…out of the overflow of the heart the mouth speaks.

The good man brings good things out of the good stored up in him and the evil man brings evil things out of the evil stored in him" (NIV, Matthew 12.34-35). This means, a man's words are the true reflection of his heart, because in the heart is the actual person. His heart mirrors and holds the key to his essential make-up.

Biblically, the heart is the source of how one speaks and lives. It constitutes the springs of life and produces its own lenses through which it sees the world. Jeremiah, the prophet says, *"The heart is so deceitful above all things and beyond cure. Who can understand it?"* (NIV, Jeremiah 17.9).

Based on this, Leslie outlined five indicators of an evil heart.

- An evil heart is expert in creating confusion and contention.
- An evil heart is an expert in fooling others with smooth speeches.

- An evil heart craves for control over others.
- An evil heart rejects feedback and accountability.
- An evil heart plays on the sympathies of good-willed people, often trumping the grace card. It demands mercy from others but gives none to them. It demands warmth, forgiveness and intimacy from others, but with no empathy for the pain it causes to others.

"We are products of our past, but we don't have to be prisoners of it" (Rick Warren).

As South Sudanese, much of our experiences have been war experiences. These have formed within us attitudes of arrogance and violence. Adults and our youth alike have developed a character of hostility and confrontation as a result of a long life spent in war. But we should not let the past experiences control or lead our future. It is now time for a positive change. As Gautama Buddha says, "No one saves us but ourselves. No one can and no one may. We ourselves must walk the path". Buddha for sure is not talking about "salvation" in Christian context but as a political, social and military agitator. He wanted his people to stand up and work hard for their nation's prosperity.

It is a fact that South Sudan is one of Africa's longest fighting nations. Most African countries have at one time fought a civil war for their political independence, followed by other inter-tribal wars for domination. But then after civilization, many political leaders have changed their approaches to governance and the settlement of conflicts among politicians. Now they prefer the way of dialogue to solve political and social conflicts. Love, respect and tolerance took precedence in the lives of the people.

Human value, rights and dignity all are highly honored. Armed struggles or uses of firearms to kill and destroy properties are not the means to solve problems. Civilized people stopped that destructive way some years ago. But this is not so with us in South Sudan. Since the 1950s, South Sudanese have been, and we are still fighting for different reasons. Some reasons are quite minor. They do not deserve human blood to be shed before ratifying them. Out of other political uproar, at least two major civil wars were fought in South Sudan for political, economic, religious, social and cultural reasons.

The paradox is that even after the two major wars for political reasons were partially resolved; tribal wars continued during those interludes. And another major civil and ethnic war broke out in 2013, which has shattered thousands and thousands of real South Sudanese family people right up to date.

> Out of other political uproar, at least two major civil wars were fought in South Sudan for political, economic, religious, social and cultural reasons.

Why did we fight?

Here I am taking our minds back to the two major political wars South Sudanese fought to attain political and economic freedom from the Democratic Republic of Sudan. South Sudan fought wars since the 1950s because there were issues which round table discussions failed to resolve. The political and economic rights of citizenship as well as development in imbalances were a great gulf between the fighting parties. The repeated wars were the last resorts to try to settle those issues because the diplomatic dialogue processes had failed.

The wars in South Sudan were natural human responses to pressures created by the Khartoum government through its inhuman treatment of the South Sudanese people. The wars came under different leadership and names but the main object was always the same. Ochieng correctly stated in his book titled "Building a New and Prosperous Society in Southern Sudan in the Post Conflict Period" that one of the most important ideological bases of the struggle by the Sudan People's Liberation Movement/ Army (SPLM/A) was to create a New Sudan. But the question is, what do we mean by create a New Sudan?

It surely means the ideological and philosophical tenants of the SPLM/A, which aim at changing and transforming the society in which citizens are liberated from a decadent old Sudan. The old Sudan leadership's main objective was to accumulate wealth, manipulate the poor people in the name of religion and Arab chauvinism. The SPLA aimed to liberate Sudan from that kind of leadership, which even now uses political Islam as a means to rule the country of Sudan; such that the new leadership that will come up will set a system which will regard the ordinary Sudanese and maintain focus on good governance and service delivery (2007, 12, 24).

Henceforth the SPLM/A envisioned itself to be the vehicle for a national transformation in Sudan. It was never seen as a struggle that would selfishly distribute positions and powers to its members for fighting in the bush.

We fought to redress Economic Inequality

An economy is an area of production, distribution or trade, with consumption of goods and services by different agents, in each geographical location. The economic agents can be individuals, businesses, organizations or governments. Transactions occur when two parties agree to the value or price of the transacted goods or services, commonly valued in a certain currency.

An economic inequality is the difference found in various measures of economic well-being, among individuals or group. Economic inequality is called income inequality. Economic disparity metrics are said to be wealth, income, and consumption.

Sudan during these times was considered as one of the most socially unequal countries in the world. The region had easy access to the basics for human needs plus extra services such as electricity, water, good roads, medical care and so forth. While in the South of Sudan, things were totally the opposite. The South Sudanese were heard being referred to as second class citizens by the Northerners.

Therefore, it was this economic discrimination, which the SPLM wanted to correct and improve. That is why, in

the Transitional Constitution, improving
the economy of the country became a
principal objective. The SPLM
government set strategies that are stated
below:

- Eradicate poverty by attaining the
  Millennium Development goals and
  guaranteeing equitable distribution
  of wealth to all states of South
  Sudan.
- Redress imbalances of income
  through achieving a decent standard
  of life for all the people of South
  Sudan.
- Empower all levels of government to
  develop and regulate their economy
  in order to achieve prosperity
  through policies aimed at increasing
  production, creating an efficient and
  self-reliant economy. And
  encouraging the free market, while
  prohibiting monopoly.
- Protect and ensure the sustainable
  management and utilization of

natural resources such as land, water, petroleum, minerals, fauna and flora, for the benefit of all the people.

- Facilitate development of the private sector, particularly indigenous entrepreneurs, to establish and develop a viable private sector capable of participating effectively in reconstruction and development.

- Encourage private initiative and self-reliance, and take all necessary steps to involve the people in the formulation and implementation of development plans and programs that affect them, and as well to enhance their right to equal opportunities in development.

- Promote agricultural, industrial and technological development by adopting appropriate policies and legislation for the encouragement and attraction of local and foreign investment.

- Take necessary measures to bring about balanced, integrated and equitable development of different areas, and to encourage and expedite rural development as a strategy for averting urban-biased development and policies that have been responsible for the neglect of rural communities.
- Ensure that National wealth is equitably shared among all levels of the government for the welfare of the people of South Sudan.

We fought to embrace the Rule of Law.

I don't know what you want, but I know what I want and what I desire to see happening in South Sudan. I want a country full of people who observe the law and use it correctly. We fought to promote:

1. Sanctity of Rights and Freedoms

Subject to Article 189 herein, no derogation from the rights and freedoms enshrined in this Bill shall be made. The Bill of Rights shall be upheld, protected and applied by the Supreme Court and other competent courts; the Human Rights Commission shall monitor its application in accordance with this Constitution and the law.

2. Life and Human Dignity

Every person has the inherent right to life, dignity and the integrity of his or her person, which shall be protected by law. No one shall be arbitrarily deprived of his or her life.

3. Personal Liberty

Every person has the right to liberty and security of person. No person shall be subjected to arrest, detention, deprivation or restriction of his or her liberty, except for specified reasons and in accordance with procedures prescribed by law.

4. Freedom from Slavery, Servitude and Forced Labor

Slavery and the slave trade in all forms are prohibited. No person shall be held in slavery or servitude. No person shall be required to perform forced or compulsory labor, except as a penalty upon conviction by a competent court of law.

5. Equality

All people are equal before the law. All are entitled to the equal protection of the law without discrimination by race, ethnic origin, color, sex, language, religion, creed, political opinion, birth locality or social status.

6. The rights of Women

Women shall be accorded full and equal dignity as men in all spheres of life.

Enact laws to combat harmful customs and traditions which undermine the dignity and status of women and provide maternity and child care, medical care for pregnant and lactating women.

Women shall have the right to own property.

7.   The right of the child

Every child has the right to all necessities to develop and mature into a full adult. These may include proper care in terms of education, health and relationships. They should not be subjected to exploitative practices and abuse.

8. First citizenship

Citizenship is a right of any person in an autonomous country. It is attained via descent, birth, naturalization, marriage, adoption and choice.

Before South Sudan became an independent country, it was one of the regions in the Democratic Republic of the Sudan. Yet the people of South Sudan were not treated as first class citizens by the ruling authorities in Khartoum.

Services of basic human needs were not objectively and proportionally accorded to the people in the South.

In comparison, infrastructure development, medical services, education at the highest levels and many other necessities were delivered with high disdain to the South.

Legally, South Sudanese did get documents like passports or nationality cards, and when it came to certain rights and benefits, people were subjected to long time suffering before they were granted any success.

That marginalization however was taken seriously by the South Sudanese political leaders. Henceforth they added to the reasons of the SPLA/M manifesto for the twenty-one years of war. Some of the manifestos, extracted from the Transitional Constitution, are listed here below:

- Every person born to a South Sudanese mother or father shall have an inalienable right to enjoy South Sudanese citizenship and nationality.
- Citizenship is the basis of equal rights and duties for all South Sudanese.
- Every citizen shall enjoy all the rights guaranteed by this Constitution.
- The law shall regulate citizenship and naturalization; no naturalized citizen shall be deprived of his or her acquired citizenship except in accordance with the law.
- A South Sudanese national may acquire the nationality of another country as shall be prescribed by law.

- A non-South Sudanese may acquire the nationality of South Sudan by naturalization as shall be prescribed by law.

- The constitution went ahead to make the following statements regarding the Nature of the Bill of Rights, sanctity of Rights and freedom, as well as life and Human dignity. That,

- The Bill of Rights is a covenant among the people of South Sudan and between them and their government at every level and a commitment to respect and promote human rights and fundamental freedoms enshrined in this Constitution; it is the cornerstone of social justice, equality and democracy.

- The rights and freedoms of individuals and groups enshrined in this Bill shall be respected, upheld and promoted by all organs and agencies of Government and by all persons.

- All rights and freedoms enshrined in international human rights treaties, covenants and instruments ratified or acceded to by the Republic of South Sudan shall be an integral part of this Bill.

- This Bill of Rights shall be upheld by the Supreme Court and other competent courts and monitored by the Human Rights Commission.

Agostoni, Tarcisio: *May the State Kill.* Pauline's Publications Africa: Nairobi. 2002. Print. Anonymous, https://leadershiplicks.com/2016/11/11/dissatisfaction-2/ (accessed April 29, 2017).

Borek John, Lovett Danny and Towns Elmer. Good Book on Leadership. Nashville: Tennessee, Broadman and Holman publishers. 2005. Print.

Clinton, Mr. Robert, *Making of a Leader:* Colorado: Springs, CO 80935. NavPress Publications: 1984. Print.

Devasia, P. *Positive Attitudes for Life*: St. Paul's Press, Bandra, Mumbai: 2010. Print.

Drago, Fr.C.S. SJ. *Forgiveness for Peace:* St. Paul Press Training School. Bandra, Mumbai. 2016. Print.

Douglas, J.D. *Bible Dictionary.* Zondervan: Grand Rapids, Michigan. 1987. Print.

Doohan Leonard. *Spiritual Leadership*:
Paulines Press, New York.2007. Print.

Grudem, Wayne. *Systematic Theology*: Inter-
Varsity Press. 1994. Print.

Elwell, Walter A. *Evangelical Dictionary of
Theology*. Baker Book House: Grand Elwell
1989. Print.

Haviland, W: *Cultural Anthropology*. Forth
Worth: Harrout Brace, Press. 1993. Print.

Holy Bible: *New International Version*.
Zondervan Publishing House: Grand
Rapids, Mic Michigan. 2005. Print.

Holy Bible: *King James Version*. Zondervan
Publishing House: Grand Rapids, Michigan.
1987. Print.

Hilde, F. Johnson. *Waging Peace in Sudan*:
Sussex ACADEMIC Press: Brighton. 2011.
Print.

Kadalie, David. *Leader's Resource Kit*.
Evangel Publishing House, Nairobi: Kenya.
2006. Print.

Katto, Japheth, Wanyama, Simeon, Musaali, Miriam E.: Corporate Governance in Uganda: Fountain Publishers, Kampala. 2014. Print.

JURIST, www.jurist.org//forum/2014/01/ June 29, 2014. Online Article.

Macmillan, School *Dictionary*: Macmillan Publishers Limited. Oxford, OX4 3PP. 2005. Print.

Murphy, Dr. Joseph. *The Power of your Subconscious Mind:* Embassy Books. Fort, Mumbai. 2014. Print.

Morley, Patrick. *Seven Seasons of the Man in the Mirror*: Zondervan, Grand Rapids. 1997. Print.

Ochieng, Philip: *Building a New and Prosperous Society in Southern Sudan in the Post Conflict Period*: African Research and Resource Forum: Nairobi. 2007. Print.

 Princeton Lyman https://www.usip.org/South-Sudan-Is-There-a-Need-for-a-New-Vision (accessed April 29, 2017).

Procter, Paul. *Cambridge International Dictionary of English*. Cambridge. Print.

Salter Colin: *Issues Facing Christians in Sudan Today*. Weefour Publications, Redruth. Cornwall. 2009. Print

Tracy, Brian. *Change you thinking Change your Life*: John Wiley & Sons, Inc. 2003. Print.

Werner, Rolandn, Anderson, William, Wheeler, Andrew: *Days of Devastation, Days of Contentment*. Pauline's Publications Africa. Daughters of St. Paul, Nairobi Kenya: 2000. Print.

2001 Summer Institute in Christian Scholarship. Dallas Baptist University, July, 11, 2001. Online Article.

www.faxnews.com/world/2016/2016/04/former-south Sudan. Online Article.

https://en.wikipedia.org/wiki/*Demographics_of_South_*Sudan10/9/2016;11:45am. Online Article.

https://en. Wikipedia. *Org/wiki/2013: South _ Sudanese_political_crisis*. 15th, *Dec.2016. 19:16.* Online Article.

htt:library.ecc-platform.orga/conflicts/natural-resources. Online Article.

https://www.biblegate *way.com*. Online Article.

http://www.whatchristian wants *to know. Com (2001)*. Online Article.

http://www.jesus.org/is-god/names of Jesus 2016. Online Article

*htt://en.wikipedia.org/wiki/south_sudan_*conflict *(2013-2014)*. Online Article.

Https://www.biblegateway.com/resources /encyclopedia-of-the bible/Bible. Online Article.

www.NewsudanVision. Com. Wed.13, March, 2013; 21:35. Online Article.

www.aljazeera.com/indepth/opinion/prof ile/mehari-taddele-maru-html. Online Article

www.bahr-el-jebel-safaris.com/*TRIBES-OF-SOUTH-SUDAN-a-*summary.html10/9/2016;11:49am. Online Article.

www.SouthSudannewsagency.com. Online Article.

www.sudantribune.com/spip.php?page=imprimable&id_article=40625. Online Article.

www.ingramcontent.com/pod-product-compliance
Lightning Source LLC
Chambersburg PA
CBHW031124250726
48655CB00002B/512